Outbreak

Science Seeks Safeguards
for Global Health

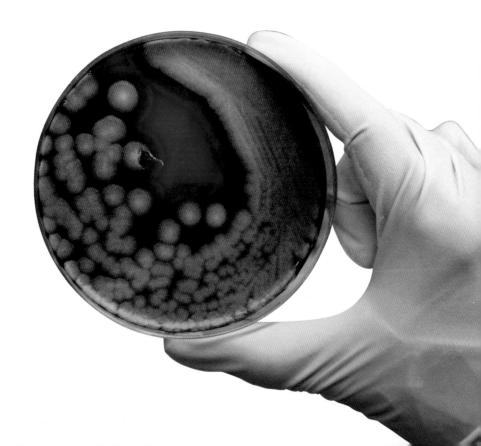

Outbreak

Science Seeks Safeguards for Global Health

By Charles Piddock
Caryn Oryniak, Consultant

NATIONAL
GEOGRAPHIC

Washington, D.C.

Contents

1 Profiling a Killer   12

Raising the dead • A global disaster • Luck strikes •
A new killer • Death from the sky • More prepared •
Species jumping • A future pandemic? • Preparing for
the worst • Creating a plan • Checklist for influenza
pandemic preparedness • Meet a microbiologist

2 The Invisible World   24

"Totally fantastic creatures" • Startling discovery •
Space invaders? • Microbiology toolbox • How
viruses work

3 A Modern Plague   30

Attack on the immune system • A continent under
siege • Vaccines • The Black Death • A new disease

4 Death From the Rain Forest   36

A deadly disease • Searching for answers • New drugs
• A medical triumph • Sharing disease

< A sign at Toronto's North York General Hospital warns people of rules regarding visitation of SARS
patients in an effort to halt the outbreak of the virus in 2003.

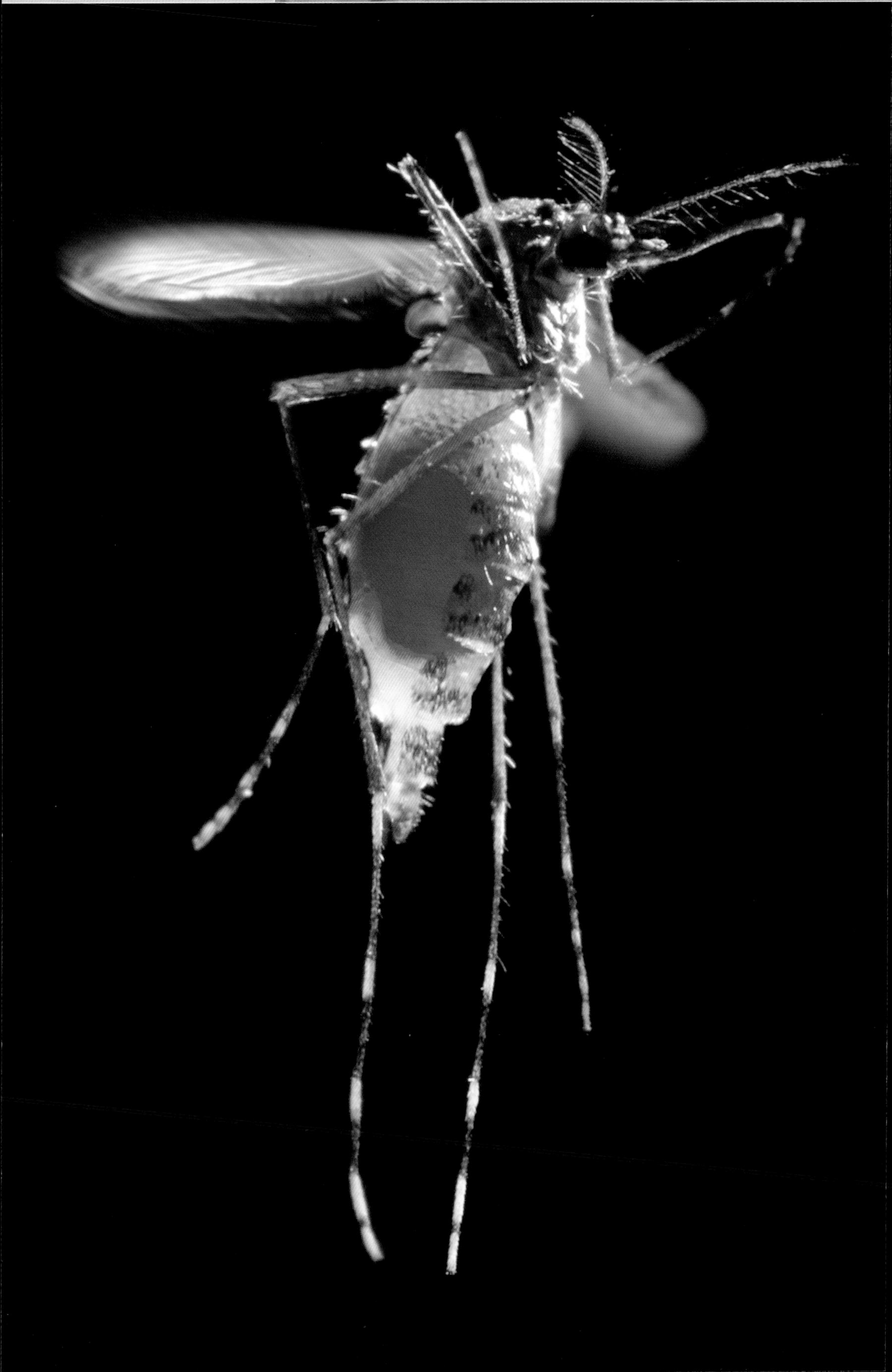

< A mosquito carries blood in her abdomen after biting her host. Mosquitoes are carriers of a number of diseases that they transmit when they break the surface of their victim's skin.

Advancements in science and technology are allowing us to combat diseases caused by viruses and bacteria like never before. This book takes you through what science is doing to help us cope with the threats from these germs. You will read about epidemics of the past and see how bacteria and viruses behave and communicate with each other, and investigate where diseases come from and how they are transmitted. You will learn about discoveries that allow us to duplicate organisms that caused devastating diseases

in the past, and explore the striking similarities these organisms have to emerging biological threats of today. This is frightening news, because the conditions today are ripe for another global outbreak. Despite a steady stream of new weapons against them, germs continue to adapt and fight back. Bacteria are becoming resistant to antibiotics, and viruses can mutate quickly. In addition to naturally emerging diseases there is also a new fear from bioterrorism. Still science and technology provide hope. We can work together to make sure we are prepared to face the future. By learning all we can about the viruses and bacteria that cause outbreaks and how they spread, we can help control these tiny organisms and prevent the world from having to suffer from another devastating global epidemic.

Caryn Oryniak
New Jersey, 2008

The Spread of the H5N1 Virus

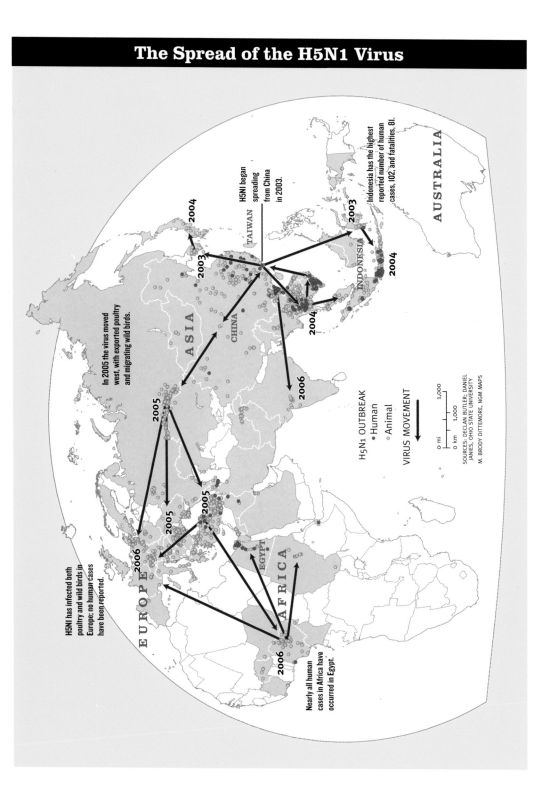

2004

TAIWAN

H5N1 began spreading from China in 2003.

2003

Indonesia has the highest reported number of human cases, 102, and fatalities, 81.

AUSTRALIA

2003

INDONESIA

2004

2004

ASIA

In 2005 the virus moved west, with exported poultry and migrating wild birds.

CHINA

2006

H5N1 OUTBREAK
- Human
- Animal

VIRUS MOVEMENT

0 mi   1,000
0 km   1,000

SOURCES: DECLAN BUTLER; DANIEL JANIES, OHIO STATE UNIVERSITY
M. BRODY DITTEMORE, NGM MAPS

2005

2005

2005

H5N1 has infected both poultry and wild birds in Europe; no human cases have been reported.

2006

EUROPE

EGYPT

AFRICA

2006

Nearly all human cases in Africa have occurred in Egypt.

Λ Scientists have been tracking H5N1 since its appearance in China in 2003. They have been careful to record both human and animal cases caused by the virus.

Bacteria

Bacteria come in three basic shapes: cocci, which are round; bacilli, which are rod-shaped; and spirilla, which are spiral-shaped.

Simple bacteria can stick together in common units, which changes their nature. A diplococcus—two rounded bacteria stuck together—causes pneumonia. Words referring to two or more bacteria stuck together to form a chain often begin with strepto–. Streptococcus is the bacterium that causes strep throat.

Words referring to bacteria stuck together in clumps or clusters often begin with staphylo-. Some serious infections, such as meningitis, can be caused by staphylococcus bacteria.

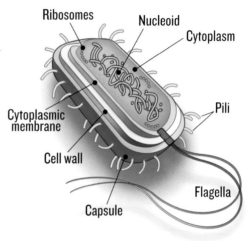

Ribosomes
Nucleoid
Cytoplasm
Cytoplasmic membrane
Pili
Cell wall
Flagella
Capsule

Timeline of Major Events Affecting Public Health

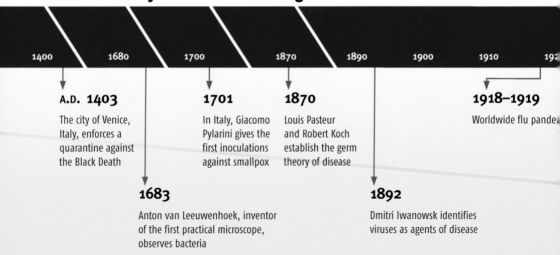

1400	1680	1700	1870	1890	1900	1910	192

A.D. 1403
The city of Venice, Italy, enforces a quarantine against the Black Death

1701
In Italy, Giacomo Pylarini gives the first inoculations against smallpox

1870
Louis Pasteur and Robert Koch establish the germ theory of disease

1918–1919
Worldwide flu pande..

1683
Anton van Leeuwenhoek, inventor of the first practical microscope, observes bacteria

1892
Dmitri Iwanowsk identifies viruses as agents of disease

Viruses

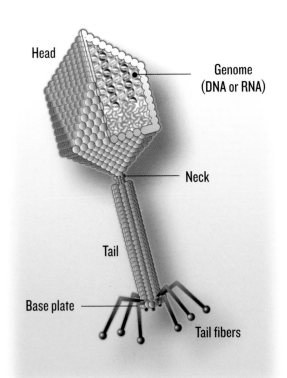

Head

Genome
(DNA or RNA)

Neck

Tail

Base plate

Tail fibers

Viruses are much smaller than bacteria. The virus that causes smallpox is one of the largest viruses. It is 1/100,000 of an inch in diameter, about one-fourth the size of an average bacterium. Influenza viruses are medium-sized, yet more than 500 can sit on the head of a pin. Other viruses are so small that a million or more could fit inside a single "o" on this page.

◁ **This virus, called a bacteriophage, kills bacteria. In Eastern Europe and Russia it is sometimes used as a substitute for antibiotics.**

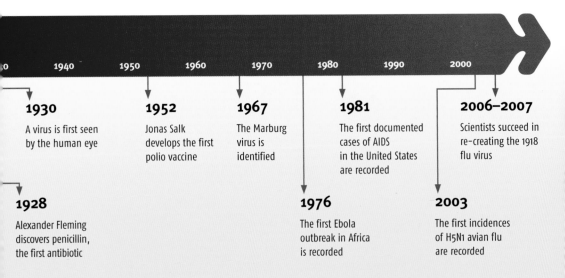

1940   1950   1960   1970   1980   1990   2000

1930

A virus is first seen by the human eye

1952

Jonas Salk develops the first polio vaccine

1967

The Marburg virus is identified

1981

The first documented cases of AIDS in the United States are recorded

2006–2007

Scientists succeed in re-creating the 1918 flu virus

1928

Alexander Fleming discovers penicillin, the first antibiotic

1976

The first Ebola outbreak in Africa is recorded

2003

The first incidences of H5N1 avian flu are recorded

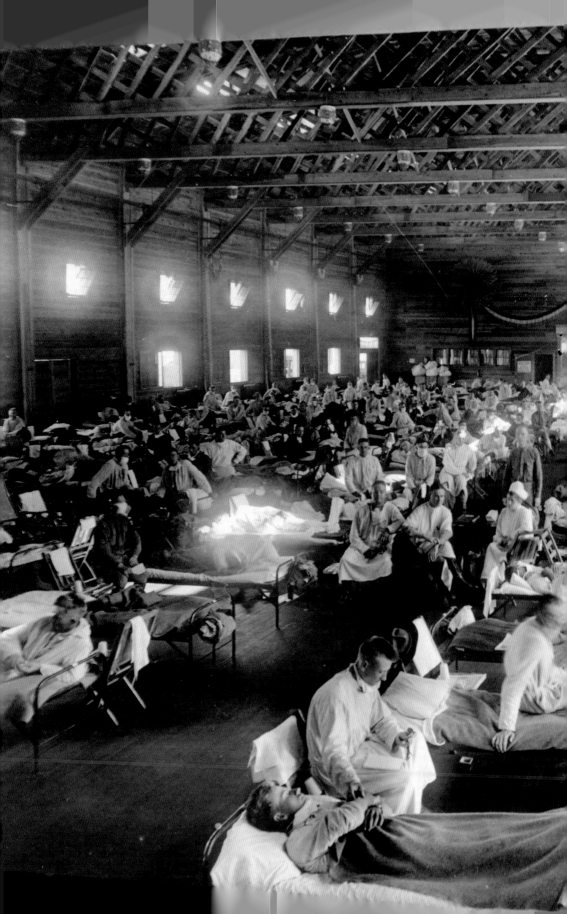

Profiling a Killer

CHAPTER 1

Science brings a long-dead virus back to life

Will it happen again? That was on the mind of Jeffrey Taubenberger in 1995 after he read a book about the 1918–1919 influenza (flu) pandemic. The virus that caused the widespread epidemic had swept the world, killing an estimated 50 million people. Most were healthy adults, struck down quickly in the prime of life. Experts consider the 1918 pandemic the worst biological disaster in modern history.

To Taubenberger, a microbiologist at the U.S. Armed Forces Institute of Pathology in Washington, D.C., the answer to his question was extremely important.

< A makeshift hospital is set up at Camp Funston, Kansas, in 1918 to serve the increasing numbers of people afflicted by the influenza epidemic.

He believed that a present-day influenza virus, H5N1, an avian (bird) flu virus, was similar to the 1918 flu virus and just might be waiting for the right conditions to spread. If a sample of the 1918 virus could be found and compared to H5N1, scientists would be better able to understand how H5N1 might mutate, or change, into a killer like the 1918 virus. That would give scientists important information about how to develop a vaccine that could save the lives of millions.

< The influenza virus as seen under the lens of an electron microscope

The team searched the institute's collection of preserved tissue samples from soldiers who died during World War I (1914–1918). After looking at 78 tissue samples, Taubenberger was able to find small fragments of the 1918 flu virus in two samples. His team also located some small virus fragments in preserved tissue samples from Britain's Royal London Hospital.

The fragments were a hopeful start, but the team needed a lot more information. The samples contained parts of only five of the virus's eight genes.

Raising the Dead

There was a rather large problem, however. How could Taubenberger find a sample of the 1918 virus? The virus disappeared when the last victim of the pandemic died. And all the 1918 victims had been buried for more than 75 years. Modern scientists need only a relatively small sample of preserved genetic material to re-create simple genes, the building codes of life. Luckily, a virus has a very simple gene structure: only eight genes, compared to the many thousands of genes that humans have. But Taubenberger's team still needed something to start with—at least a piece of preserved genetic structure from the 1918 virus. If they could find that, it might be possible to re-create the virus in a laboratory.

∧ A preserved specimen of lung tissue containing fragments of the 1918 flu virus has enabled scientists to decode the genetic structure of this microscopic killer.

A Global Disaster

It struck violently, wiping out babies in their cribs, old people in their beds, and young women and men in the prime of their lives. People who felt fine in the morning were dead by night, so quickly did the 1918 flu virus take lives. One doctor wrote in 1918 of people with seemingly ordinary flu symptoms rapidly developing "the most vicious type of pneumonia that has ever been seen" and then "struggling for air until they suffocate."

Experts say that it is likely that one billion people contracted the disease between 1918 and 1919 and that at least 50 million people died from it. The real death toll, however, may have been twice as high since highly populated areas in Asia and Africa may have underreported the number of deaths. The flu killed people on every continent except Antarctica.

In the United States, 20 million Americans became infected and an estimated 500,000 died—ten times the number of U.S. soldiers killed in World War I. In a useless effort to stop the spread of the disease, many towns and cities closed theaters, churches, and other public areas. Laws made it illegal to spit, cough, or even sneeze in public. In New York City, those who did so faced fines of up to $500. When people ventured outdoors, they covered their mouths and noses with masks. The deadly disease disappeared almost as fast as it had spread without anyone understanding why. Within 18 months, people stopped dying, and the entire world mourned its dead.

∧ In Bordeaux, France, the coffin carrying an American soldier who died of influenza is escorted to the funeral site by members of the soldier's unit.

The new samples promised to provide enough clues to reconstruct the virus's missing three genes. Now, Taubenberger's team could set out to sequence, or map, the genes of the entire 1918 virus—a necessary first step to re-creating it in a laboratory. It took months of work and the use of powerful computers loaded with advanced software to analyze millions of bits of information. The team finally succeeded in determining the virus's sequence of genes. Taubenberger now had the biological blueprints needed to actually re-create the 1918 mass killer.

A New Killer

Taubenberger then sent the sequence information to Peter Palese and his team of scientists at New York's Mount Sinai School of Medicine. Using a technique called reverse genetics, the Mount Sinai team followed the sequence, called a code, to create microscopic, virus-like strings of genes called plasmids. They then sent the plasmids to a third team of scientists at the U.S. Centers for Disease Control and Prevention (CDC) in Atlanta, Georgia. Researchers there inserted the plasmids into human kidney cells grown in a laboratory to start the process of recreating the actual killer virus itself. "Once you get the plasmids inside the cell, the virus assembles itself," said Terrence Tumpey, the CDC research scientist who put the virus together. "It takes only a couple of days."

∧ Pathologists Jeffrey Taubenberger (*left*) and Johan Hultin pay their respects at a memorial to victims of the 1918 flu epidemic in Mission, Alaska.

Luck Strikes

Then luck intervened. Johan Hultin, a 72-year-old retired doctor, happened to read about Taubenberger's efforts. In 1951, Hultin had recovered fragments of the 1918 virus from a mass grave in Brevig Mission, Alaska, a tiny settlement hugging the shore of the frigid Bering Sea. The bodies had been buried in permanently frozen ground, so they were extremely well preserved. Hultin went back to Brevig Mission and dug up the corpse of a female flu victim. He extracted samples of tissue from her lungs and sent them to Taubenberger.

Tumpey confirmed what Taubenberger and others suspected but had not conclusively proved: the 1918 virus was an avian flu virus very similar to H5N1. He found this out by injecting the re-created virus into fertilized bird eggs. The virus killed the eggs, just as H5N1 kills them. Other modern-day flu virus strains that are human-to-human viruses do not kill fertilized bird eggs.

V Health officials collect dead chickens in Hong Kong's New Territories. More than half a million birds were slaughtered in the region in an effort to stop the spread of the deadly avian virus.

Death From the Sky

No one knows exactly where H5N1 originated. One guess is that it became a mutated virus infecting flocks of migrating wild birds, then spread to domestic flocks of chickens and turkeys in China. Around 2003, farmers in southern China and southeastern Asia noticed that their flocks were rapidly dying off. The bird disease quickly spread throughout eastern Asia, into Turkey and Russia, then on to Europe as far as England. By 2007, more than 100 million chickens, turkeys, and ducks had perished from the virus and millions more were destroyed by health officials trying to stop the spread of the virus.

More Prepared

Thanks to the research of three scientific teams, scientists are now able to study the reconstructed 1918 virus. They can examine its structure and compare it to known versions of bird and human influenza viruses. The increasing information on H5N1 can be fed into a computer to create a model of how the virus mutates, or changes. Computer models can then be compared to how the virus operates in real life. What the scientists have learned already has confirmed suspicions that H5N1 has a powerful potential to mutate into a virus like the one that struck in 1918. The new knowledge allows scientists to predict what might happen next to the virus and to prepare the world for it.

∧ Poultry samples are tested for evidence of avian or bird flu.

∨ Statistics from the 1918-1919 influenza are discussed by Anthony S. Fauci, the Director of the National Institute of Allergy and Infectious Diseases in 2005, at a conference focusing on the consequences of an outbreak of avian flu.

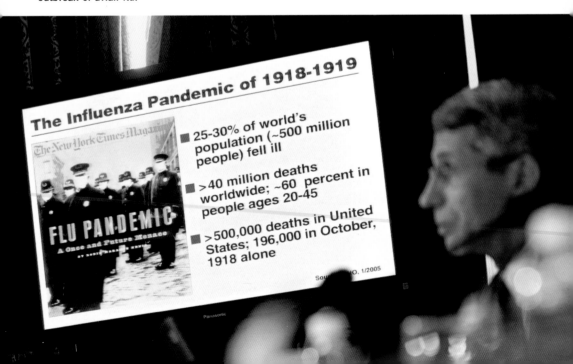

The Influenza Pandemic of 1918-1919

The New York Times Magazine

FLU PANDEMIC
A Once and Future Menace

- 25-30% of world's population (~500 million people) fell ill
- >40 million deaths worldwide; ~60 percent in people ages 20-45
- >500,000 deaths in United States; 196,000 in October, 1918 alone

Source: WHO, 1/2005

Species Jumping

Most flu viruses attack only one species, but H5N1 is different. It has shown an ability to jump from one species to another: attacking birds, pigs, goats, and even flies. H5N1 also strikes quickly. A bird can be sitting on a bench, apparently healthy, and then suddenly fall over dead.

Humans have also contracted influenza from H5N1. Since the outbreak was first noticed in 1993, about 60 people have died, mostly in Vietnam, but also in Cambodia, Thailand, Indonesia, and Egypt. All these deaths apparently occurred when the virus jumped from birds to humans.

A Future Pandemic?

What worries health officials most, however, is the threat that a new mutation will allow the virus to jump directly from human to human. That is what scientists believe took place in 1918. For that to occur again, H5N1 would have to first mutate into another strain. It could happen this way: A human infected with H5N1 from a bird also becomes infected with a human flu virus. Inside the person's body, the two viruses begin to share the same genetic material, thus giving birth to a new and more deadly strain of virus— one as contagious as human influenza and as deadly as bird flu. This new virus would have the ability to jump directly from human to human. "If the virus becomes highly contagious

among humans, the health impact in terms of deaths...will be enormous," said Shigeru Omi of the World Health Organization (WHO). The United Nations public health agency predicts that 2 million to 50 million people could die of such a disease. "The world is now in the gravest danger of a pandemic," Omi said.

∧ A staff member at the Office of Health and Safety at the Centers for Disease Control and Prevention in Atlanta poses in a protective suit that includes a respirator. Field researchers wear this suit when investigating highly infectious diseases like Ebola or Marburg.

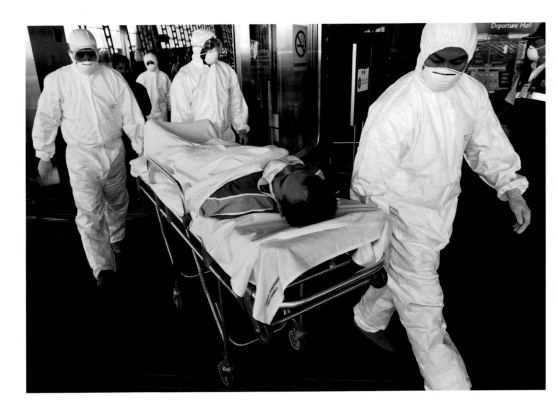

∧ A "victim" is escorted on a stretcher through Kuala Lumpur International Airport in Sepang, Malaysia, in January 2008 during exercises preparing officials in the event of a possible influenza epidemic in the country.

Preparing for the Worst

Though H5N1 might never mutate into a killer human virus, researchers around the globe are racing to prepare for the worst. John Oxford, a world-renowned virus expert at Queen Mary's School of Medicine in Great Britain, thinks it is only a question of time before H5N1 becomes a dangerous killer of humans. Oxford also believes that it will take more than medication and vaccines to manage a pandemic in modern times. It will take a change of attitude. In November of 2006, Oxford stated, "It's going to be exceedingly difficult for these modern societies to contend with [an] outbreak, when it comes. ....I think these modern societies will be on the verge of panic, given the first pandemic of the 21st century.... That's why it is so important to prepare." Oxford is just one of the researchers studying how societies around the globe will react to a pandemic. His research involves collecting stories from relatives of those who died in the 1918 pandemic in an attempt to reconstruct and theorize modern behavior. It is hoped that this time, however, humankind—thanks to cooperative scientific research—will be better equipped to fight the killer, unlike what happened in 1918 and 1919, when the world was caught by surprise.

Creating a Plan

The World Health Organization has estimated that an influenza epidemic could result in more than two million deaths around the world, with the largest impact felt in developing nations. A pandemic could occur when a particular flu virus mutates and becomes a germ for which current vaccines cannot provide immunity. The WHO has laid out guidelines for coping with an influenza pandemic. Unfortunately, countries with limited resources will have a more difficult time managing outbreaks.

Preparations for a pandemic include managing the smaller yearly outbreaks that affect small pockets of the population. By staying on top of minor changes in the flu virus and following an aggressive vaccination program, it may be possible to stay a step ahead of a pandemic. Additionally, countries are advised to develop plans for alerting the general public, something which will be harder to accomplish in less developed nations where segments of the population are isolated and uneducated. The WHO also advises countries to stockpile vaccines and invest in research and production of medications within their own countries.

Checklist for Influenza Pandemic Preparedness

Health officials are advised to create flu response plans according to the following categories:

- Preparing for an emergency
- Surveillance
- Case investigation and treatment
- Preventing spread of disease within the community
- Maintaining essential health services
- Research and evaluation
- Implementation, testing, and revision of the national plan

Source: *World Health Organization*

Λ An airport employee wears a mask to protect herself against possible infection during an exercise designed to safeguard the population against viral outbreaks at Kuala Lumpur International Airport in Malaysia in January 2008.

Meet a Microbiologist

Terrence Tumpey is a research microbiologist at the Centers for Disease Control (CDC) in Atlanta, Georgia. His work has led to a greater level of readiness in the event of a modern-day influenza pandemic.

What do you find is the most challenging part of your job?

Believe it or not, the most challenging part of my job is not the actual research. That is certainly challenging. But it is often a challenging job simply to get approval to do research. This was particularly true in reconstructing the 1918 virus. We had to present our research plan through a number of committees. CDC's Biosafety Committee had to approve the research because the virus is so deadly. We had to make sure there was no chance it would escape the laboratory and reinfect the world. We also had to get approved by the Animal Care and Use Committee. That committee makes sure that animals used in experiments are given good treatment.

In addition to these safeguards, the CDC laboratories are inspected each year by the U.S. Department of Agriculture and another CDC Office of Safety and Health.

Once all those committees had approved the research, we could go ahead. The results of our research had to be reviewed again at CDC and then we submitted our results to peer review outside of CDC. Peer review is a review of your experiment and results by other leading researchers in the field. Once peer review was done, we could go ahead and publish our findings.

This process demonstrates an important part of scientific research: It is a job done by many people, not just the scientist in the lab working alone. Cooperation and sharing data are essential. The thrill of scientific discovery is often a team feeling.

What is the most rewarding part of your job?

In general, the most rewarding part of my job is to work with young, enthusiastic graduate students. It's especially satisfying to see their progress in the field of microbiology or virology. Virology, of course, is the study of viruses.

As a child, were you interested in becoming a microbiologist? If not, what did you want to be?

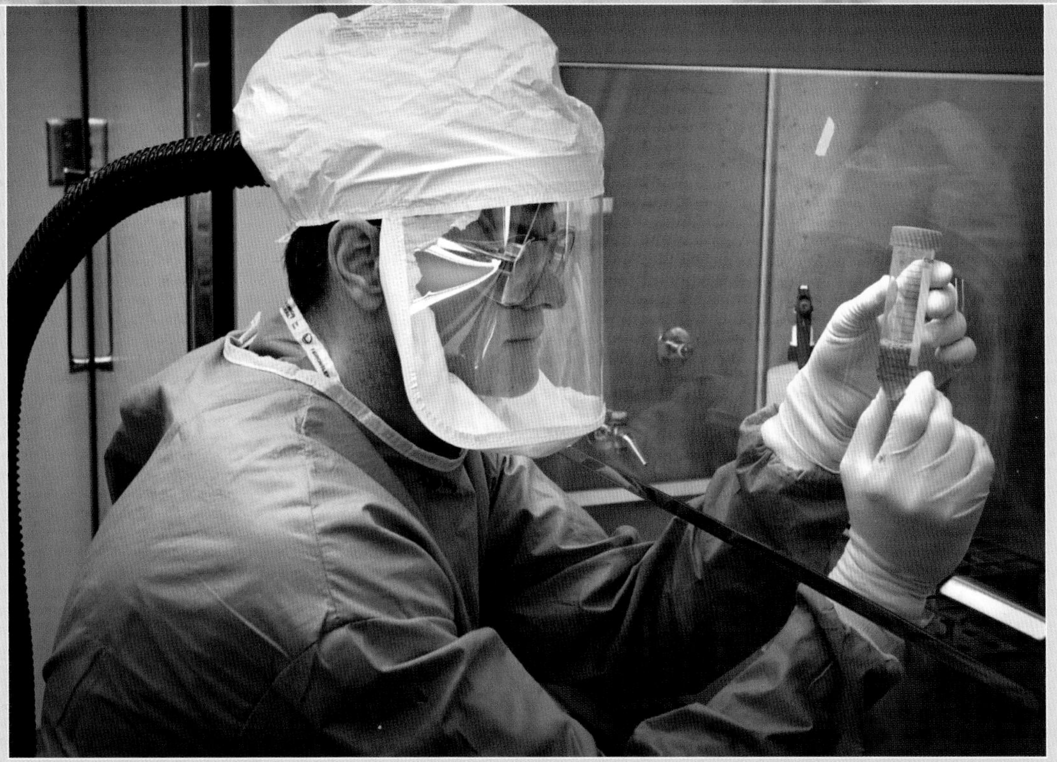

Dr. Terrence Tumpey examines a re-created 1918 influenza virus specimen made visible inside the vial with an orange dye.

A I did not think about becoming a scientist until I started college. It was then that I realized I needed to declare a major. I selected biology since it was the one class in high school where I obtained straight A's. I figured it was a sign that I was destined to become a microbiologist. Actually, as a child growing up (and even today), I wanted to be a baseball player. I wanted to play for the Chicago Cubs. I'm still a loyal fan. Someday, they're going to be world champions.

Q How would you rate the importance of the research you are doing for global health?

A In general, we are using the reconstructed 1918 virus as a model to better understand other influenza viruses that could cause widespread damage, such as the virus responsible for bird flu. These experiments will help us understand the biological and molecular properties that made the 1918 pandemic influenza virus so deadly. Our research will also help scientists design better ways of halting the spread of dangerous influenza viruses. Because research is generally a slow process, the benefits of rescuing the 1918 virus will not be obvious for a number of years.

Q What would you tell a young person interested in becoming a research scientist? What does it take?

A I think research is fun and exciting and the thrill of discovery is a feeling unlike any other. At this point, I could not imagine doing anything else. When I applied to Ph.D. programs, most did not require a Master of Science degree. That allows undergraduates who apply to go straight into these programs. Also, you don't have to be the smartest person in the world to get a Ph.D. What you need is just to be passionate about a particular area of study. And you need to work hard.

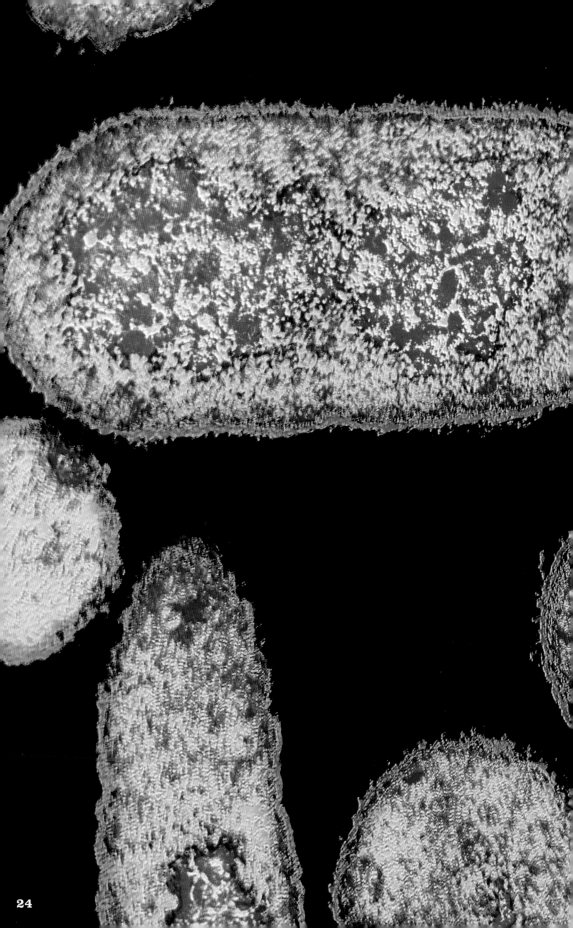

The Invisible World

CHAPTER 2

Microbes are everywhere

It is probably a good thing that viruses and bacteria are too small to see with just the human eye. Otherwise, life might resemble a horror show. Everywhere—in the air, on the ground, in the water, and, worst of all, on your face and body—you would see swarms of swirling, wiggling, floating, crawling, nasty-looking things.

More than 100 trillion microscopic creatures, most of them bacteria and viruses, live just on the outside of an average human body. Inside your body, swimming in your bloodstream, attaching to your cells, and floating in your stomach and intestines, there are many trillions more. Scientists say that

< E. coli bacteria normally reside in the body, but under certain conditions can cause a fatal infection.

the average human body carries around ten times more microbes than it has cells.

"Totally Fantastic Creatures"

It might be hard for the average person to think of bacteria with much fondness—especially since bacteria cause many of humankind's most feared diseases. For example, bacteria are responsible for cholera, tuberculosis, and bubonic plague.

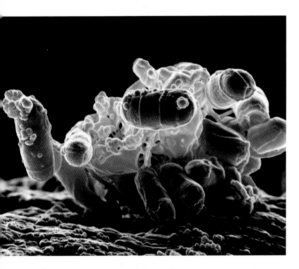

∧ A cluster of E. coli bacteria as seen through an electron microscope

Bonnie Bassler, however, thinks bacteria are fascinating. Bassler is an associate professor of molecular biology at Princeton University. As an undergraduate in California, she wanted to become a veterinarian. But there was one problem: Dissections in biology class made her faint. Then she volunteered to work in a biochemistry lab. "I was planning

to cure cancer," she said; "then I discovered that bacteria were these totally fantastic creatures."

Bacteria are seemingly simple creatures, but they are about as tough as life can get. Scientists now believe that bacteria have been on earth for about three and a half billion years. During that time, they have adapted to all different kinds of environments, even those that would kill every other form of life. Bacteria are found inside glaciers, in the boiling water of hot springs, and in the dark, pressurized murk of the ocean floor. Some types of bacteria do not even need oxygen, and others can live indefinitely encased in hardened shells.

Even though bacteria have no nervous system, they respond to changes in their environment. They can sense food and move toward it. They seem to be able to remember for as long as 60 seconds, which is a long time in the life of a bacterium.

Startling Discovery

In 2006, Bassler and other researchers at Princeton discovered something seemingly unbelievable about bacteria: They actually talk to each other. They communicate not with sound, but with molecules similar to pheromones. Pheromones are chemicals widely used in the animal world for communication.

Bassler's research team found that disease-causing bacteria, when they have multiplied in the body to a certain point, send out a signal. The signal says, in effect, "There's enough of us now to do some real damage. Let's go!" The discovery, which has given Bassler the nickname "the bacteria whisperer," could give doctors a powerful weapon in the battle against bacteria-caused disease. If bacterial language can be understood, scientists might find ways to disrupt communication. If bacteria cannot talk to each other, they might remain harmless, unable to cause disease.

Today, medical science fights bacterial infections mainly with antibiotics, substances that kill harmful bacteria without harming cells. New antibiotics must constantly be developed because bacteria mutate into forms that are not harmed by existing antibiotics, creating resistant "superbugs" that cannot be killed. A new way to fight bacteria, even the superbugs, might emerge through chemicals that disrupt the way bacteria talk to each other.

Space Invaders?

Bacteria, like humans, are living creatures that eat, multiply, and seem to have some social interaction. Viruses, however, by themselves, cannot do any of those things—which has led some scientists to question whether they can even be classified as living creatures. Some viruses are shaped like long, thin rods. Others look like soft, fluffy cotton balls.

Still others look like multisided crystals. The virus that causes the common cold looks like a soccer ball made of 20 closely fitted triangles. Outside a cell, a virus appears to be nothing more than a collection of DNA (deoxyriboneucleic acid) or RNA (ribonucleic acid) surrounded by a coat of protein. Both DNA and RNA are molecules that contain genetic information in the form of a code. So, in effect, a virus is a packet of coded information in a protective capsule.

Viruses are so odd compared to ordinary living things that some scientists have speculated that they may have arrived from space, crashing to earth hundreds of millions, if not billions, of years ago.

V **The view through an electron microscope shows human blood cells (*green*) infected with the human immunodeficiency virus (HIV) (*red*).**

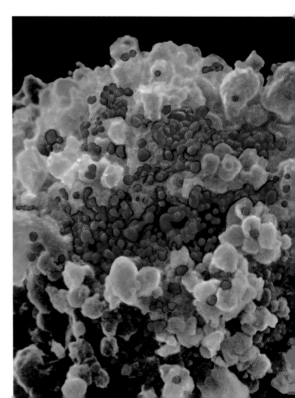

Microbiology Toolbox

Microbiologists use a number of high-tech tools to study bacteria, viruses, and other microbes. First, scientists must culture, or grow, bacteria and viruses so they can multiply in a laboratory setting. Once they have cultured a good sample of microbes, researchers prepare them to be clearly seen. Seeing microbes is made easier by staining them. There are many types of stains. Some are colored dyes that can be absorbed by a microbe, turning it green or red. Scientists also use epifluorescent stains, which are absorbed into the microbe's DNA, causing it to glow when seen through a microscope.

Microbiologists also use different types of microscopes. Optical microscopes can magnify a microbe up to 1,000 times. This magnification is enough to see most bacteria, but not viruses and not the material deep inside bacteria. In order to see viruses, microbiologists use electron microscopes. Instead of using light rays, electron microscopes shoot a stream of electrons toward an object. Researchers then view the object on a computer screen at magnifications of tens of thousands.

While using microscopes to look at microbes has given them much valuable information, researchers are turning more and more to DNA analysis of microbes, using machines called gene sequencers. Powerful computer programs enable scientists to analyze genes and their very complex chemical interactions. They allow scientists to compare the code on millions of bits of DNA in order to understand how bacteria and viruses grow, develop, mutate and, in the case of disease germs, attack.

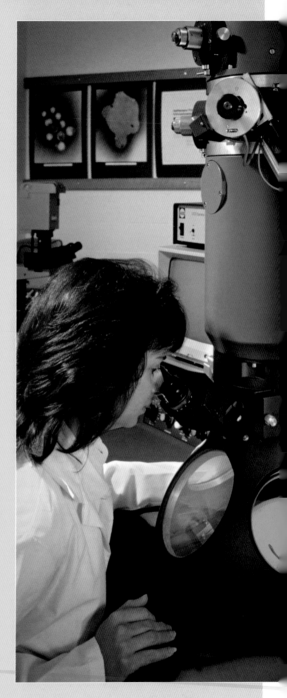

∧ A microbiologist works at an electron microscope at the Centers for Disease Control and Prevention in Atlanta, Georgia.

How Viruses Work

Once inside the body, some viruses just float about harmlessly, doing nothing. Others, such as the virus that causes the common cold, do their damage immediately. Still other viruses can lurk in the body for years and then spring into action. All viruses need to attach themselves to cells in order to function. They either break through the cell's wall or they somehow fool the cell into thinking that they are part of the cell's normal food.

Once inside the cell, viruses chemically fool the cell into using the virus's, not the cell's, genetic material to produce more viruses. In this way, they spread through the body, attacking more cells and producing more viruses.

What triggers an inactive virus into action? The answer is still a mystery, and scientists are looking for the answer.

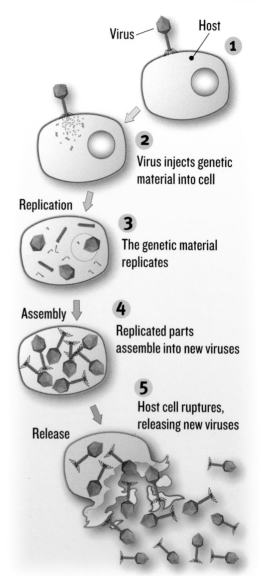

Virus — Host

1

2
Virus injects genetic material into cell

Replication

3
The genetic material replicates

Assembly

4
Replicated parts assemble into new viruses

5
Host cell ruptures, releasing new viruses

Release

∧ How a virus reproduces (replicates) is shown above. The steps in the process are: 1) attack, 2) entry, 3) reproduction, 4) assembly, and 5) release.

< Streptococcus pneumonia bacteria, pictured here, are commonly found in the nose and throat. The bacteria are responsible for common illnesses such as strep throat and more menacing infections like meningitis.

A Modern Plague

CHAPTER 3

Science looks for a cure for AIDS

Large areas of the world are now in the death grip of a killer disease that claims more lives each year. The disease is acquired immune deficiency syndrome (AIDS), caused by a virus called human immunodeficiency virus (HIV). The figures are startling: The number of people living with HIV worldwide has risen from about 8 million in 1990 to nearly 40 million today. In 2006 alone, an estimated 4.3 million people contracted HIV and 2.9 million people died of complications from AIDS.

< Patients suffering from HIV infection wait to be treated for tuberculosis, a bacterial disease that in most healthy people, would likely remain inactive. HIV compromises the body's ability to fight off infections.

Attack on the Immune System

HIV is a virus that directly attacks the body's immune system—the body's main defense against disease. If a hostile virus or bacterium enters the body through the skin or in some other way, it is likely to encounter trillions of lymphocytes, or white blood cells. The lymphocytes prowl the bloodstream and other body areas, like soldiers looking for invaders. When one is discovered, special lymphocytes called B cells and T cells help make antibodies—custom chemicals that attack and destroy the invader. Each antibody destroys only a specific germ. If a chicken pox virus, for instance, invades the body, the immune system makes an antibody to destroy that kind of chicken pox virus. The antibody is useless against any other type of virus. B cells and T cells

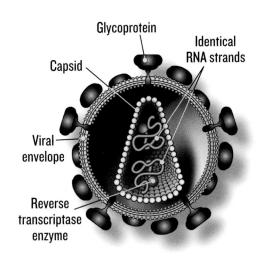

∧ The HIV virus (*above*) attacks T-cells, preventing them from producing the antibodies needed to fight infection.

also produce memory cells, so that, after the threat is gone, the body will recognize and attack a future invasion of that same virus.

HIV, however, attacks T cells themselves, so they cannot recognize invaders and make antibodies. A person with HIV gradually loses the ability to fight infections, resulting in acquired immune deficiency syndrome (AIDS), the most advanced HIV disease. Over a period of time, people sicken and die from infections they would ordinarily be able to fight off.

A Continent Under Siege

All areas of the world have been hit by the AIDS epidemic, but Africa has suffered the most. In Africa,

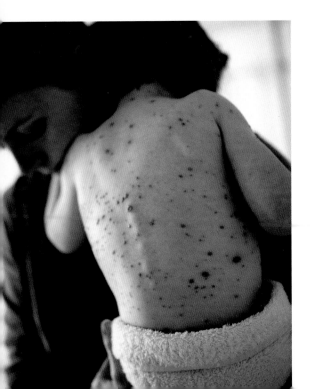

< A child with chicken pox, an illness caused by the varicella-zoster virus, is comforted by her mother. Chicken pox sores typically cover the trunk of the body but can also appear in the nose and throat.

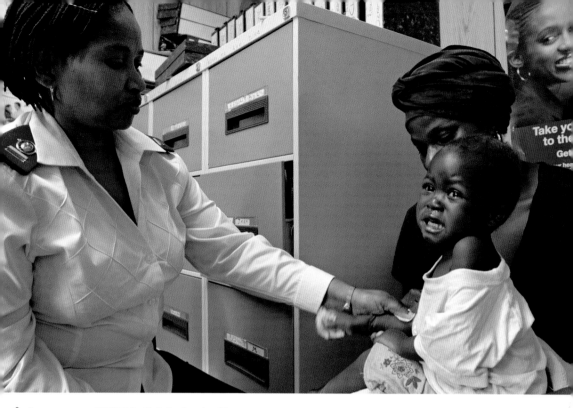

∧ A nurse at an HIV/AIDS clinic in South Africa treats a child suffering from the disease.

an estimated 24.7 million people are now living with HIV/AIDS, making up 63 percent of all the cases worldwide. There are more than 12 million AIDS orphans in Africa—children who have lost both parents to the disease.

Medical science is looking for a way to stop or slow this epidemic. The most intense search is for a vaccine—a substance made from killed or weakened viruses or bacteria that causes the body to develop antibodies against attack without causing the disease itself. Vaccines have already been developed to inoculate people against a number of viruses. But HIV, because of its ability to mutate quickly, has proved impossible to make into a vaccine so far.

Vaccines

Modern medicine's main weapon against viruses is vaccines. A vaccine is a weakened or dead form of a disease that is introduced into the body through a shot, or by mouth. The virus in the vaccine is not strong enough to cause disease, but it is strong enough to activate the body's immune system. It is somewhat like showing the immune system a "Wanted" poster. Then, if the real virus enters the body, the immune system recognizes it immediately and attacks, destroying the virus. Without a vaccine, the immune system does not recognize the virus intruder, so the virus is free to multiply, often overwhelming the body and causing illness, before the immune system can react properly.

The Black Death

The most devastating plague in history was the Black Death. It began in 1348 in Italy. By the time the epidemic was finished, it had wiped out an estimated one-fourth to one-half of Europe's entire population.

Symptoms of the Black Death were ghastly: fever, aching limbs, bulbous black buboes (swollen lymph glands) that burst and oozed like rotten tomatoes, and bloody vomit. Italian writer Giovanni Boccaccio (ca. 1313–1375), who lived through the plague, wrote that the disease spread so rapidly that its victims "ate lunch with their friends and ate dinner with their ancestors in paradise."

So many people died so quickly that corpses were thrown into the streets or piled into huge burial pits. The smell was so overpowering that doctors wore beak-like masks filled with aromatic herbs when they treated the sick. Whole towns and cities lay deserted.

At the time, people did not know what caused the plague. Many believed God had created the disease to punish them. Others believed the disease was caused by an unusual arrangement of the planets, causing earth to send out deadly vapors. People tried to stop the spread of the disease by burning incense and carrying dried flowers.

Today, scientists know that the Black Death was bubonic plague, caused by the bacterium Yersinia pestis. These bacteria infected fleas that infested rats. Rats aboard ships arriving from Asia likely brought the disease to Italy. From there, they spread out into towns and villages across Europe, carrying the fleas with them. When humans were bitten by the infected fleas, they developed the disease and usually died within three days. A second variation of

the plague—pneumonic plague—attacked the lungs and was spread by just breathing the exhaled breath of a victim. Pneumonic plague killed in one or two days. As recently as 20 years ago, the city of Surat, India, was devastated by an outbreak of pneumonic plague.

∧ The costumes worn by doctors who treated plague victims in the 1700s truly prevented them from contracting the infection. The long black robes kept them from being bitten by the fleas that spread the disease, and the bizarre masks filled with aromatic oils kept doctors from becoming infected by their patients' exhaled breath.

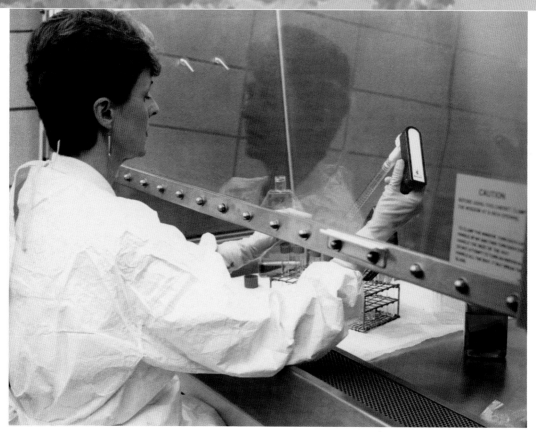

∧ A CDC researcher studies the HIV virus. Much of the funding for AIDS is directed toward finding a vaccine to prevent people from getting this virus.

After years of effort, however, scientists have developed a number of drugs that slow the progress of the disease. These drugs are proving very effective in keeping people alive. In 2007, Canadian researchers led by Eric Cohen achieved a breakthrough when they discovered that HIV has an "accomplice" in its assault on the immune system: a small protein chemical. The virus uses this protein to create an environment inside the cell that allows the virus to multiply faster. Researchers may now be able to develop a drug to disable the protein, thus further slowing down the progress of the disease.

A New Disease

AIDS is a new disease. It was not even identified until 1981, and most researchers now believe it may have jumped from chimpanzees to humans.

It is also a very fragile virus. It cannot exist outside the body for long. As a result, HIV is not transmitted through day-to-day activities such as shaking hands or hugging. HIV is most commonly transmitted through sexual contact, the sharing of hypodermic needles, and transmission from infected mothers to newborns at birth.

Death From the Rain Forest

CHAPTER 4

Deadly viruses emerge in Africa

The African rain forest has a thick covering of vegetation and swarms of creatures that bite and sting. But nothing to emerge from the rain forest in recent years is as scary and dangerous as two you cannot see. These are filoviruses—agents of diseases called Ebola (named after the Ebola River in the African country of Zaire) and Marburg (named after a town in Germany). Under the microscope, the viruses look like worms or snakes, often coiled at one end.

Marburg hit first in 1967 when African green monkeys brought to Marburg, Germany, infected

< **The green monkey, a species used in research facilities around the world, is responsible for spreading the first known outbreaks of Marburg virus. A vaccine to protect the primates has reportedly met with success.**

lab workers. Seven researchers died horrible, quick deaths in Marburg and in nearby Frankfurt. Ebola was first recorded in 1976 in Zaire, when Mabalo Lokela, a 44-year-old schoolteacher, became sick after returning to the small town of Yambuku from a trip in the north of the country. He died 14 days later. Soon, hospital workers who treated Lokela became sick. Most of the hospital staff died.

∧ Workers burying a child who died of Ebola wear protective suits to avoid being infected by the highly contagious virus.

A Deadly Disease

The symptoms of both diseases are similar. They begin abruptly with fever, headache, joint and muscle aches, sore throat, and weakness. Then most victims develop diarrhea, vomiting, and stomach pain, followed by bleeding inside and outside the body.

In the worst cases, the victims' insides turn into a kind of bloody pudding, and death follows in one or two weeks.

∧ A patient in Yambuku in the Republic of the Congo in 1976 is quarantined when it is suspected that he might have contracted Ebola.

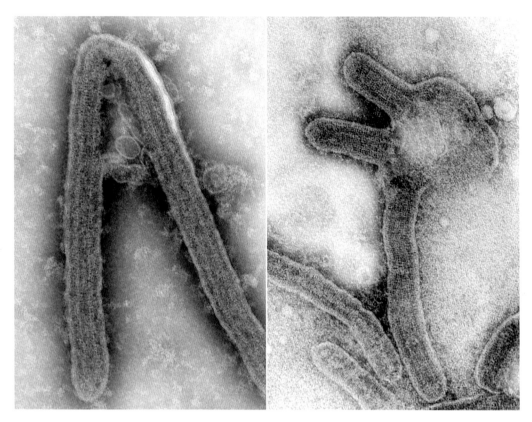

∧ The Marburg and Ebola viruses look very different under an electron microscope. The Ebola virus (*right*) takes various shapes, while the Marburg virus is rod-shaped and can fold itself up.

The first outbreak of Ebola infected 284 people, with half of them dying. A few months later, a second outbreak emerged, infecting 318 people and killing 88 percent of them. Since then, more than a thousand people have died from Ebola and several hundred from Marburg in more than 17 separate outbreaks. Those are small numbers compared to the millions who have died of AIDS. But scientists worry because the filoviruses attack so quickly and spread so easily from human to human. A major outbreak of Ebola or Marburg, spreading across Africa and into other areas of the world, is a terrifying possibility.

Searching for Answers

Scientists know what filoviruses look like and how they kill, but an important part of understanding how a virus or other germ spreads is to find out where it originates. Where is the reservoir, or breeding ground, of the virus? Often this is found in a species that carries the virus, but is not affected by it.

Scientists looked for clues about how Marburg and Ebola were transmitted to humans. During

< A field worker searching for diseased and dying animals in Odzala National Park in the Republic of the Congo wears a protective suit that filters air to remove deadly viruses.

every recent human outbreak, gorilla carcasses have turned up in nearby forests. Scientist Magdalena Bermejo of the University of Barcelona in Spain has studied the gorillas since 2002 and found that they also died from filovirus infection. In addition, Bermejo discovered that large numbers of chimpanzees were killed by the viruses. Based on the size of the infected region, Bermejo thinks that as many as 5,500 gorillas in the countries of Gabon and the Republic of Congo have been killed by the

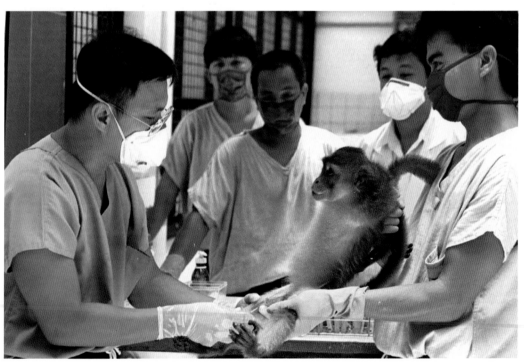

∧ A Filipino veterinarian takes blood from a sick macaque monkey in order to test for a possible Ebola virus infection. This was one of 7,000 monkeys tested on a farm in May 1996 after a primate research center in Texas traced a monkey with Ebola to a shipment from the Philippines.

diseases. She estimates that the viruses may have wiped out more than 80 percent of the local chimpanzees, too.

Still, that does not answer the question of what species is the natural reservoir for the viruses. How did the gorillas and chimps get the viruses?

In 2007, researchers in Gabon may have discovered what they were looking for. They found both the Marburg virus and the Ebola virus in African fruit bats that do not appear to be affected by the disease. Each of the three species found to harbor the viruses has migrated to areas where Ebola outbreaks have occurred, and where the local people are known to eat bats. If the fruit bat is the reservoir for the viruses, then destroying the infected bats would break the chain of infection and save the lives of humans, gorillas, and chimps. Researchers could predict "danger" spots where people and primates are most vulnerable by tracking the bats' migration patterns. Researchers warn against knee-jerk reactions such as killing off the entire fruit bat population of an affected region. Bats play an important role in the ecosystem. Education of local populations is

< An African fruit bat

believed to be the most effective way of preventing future outbreaks of Ebola.

New Drugs

Much work still has to be done, before the evidence is conclusive. Recently, an antiviral drug used on patients with leukemia was found to defend the body against the Ebola virus. Scientists have also had some success with a vaccine designed to prevent Marburg virus. The vaccine has only been tested on animals, but provides researchers with hope that someday these deadly filoviruses may be prevented.

Scientists like Dr. Bermejo believe a vaccination program to protect gorillas in the wild is a good option. It appears that among gorillas, Ebola is spread by social interaction rather than eating a host species. Vaccination would help save an endangered species and insure the economic survival of a human population that depends on wildlife for tourism. Positive results for a vaccine that protects apes against Ebola have been encouraging. Biologists and conservationists alike hope more funds are directed towards research and use of animal vaccines in the future.

A Medical Triumph

Defeating killer viral diseases such as AIDS or Ebola may seem like an impossible task. But researchers can take heart from one of medicine's greatest victories. Fifty years ago, the most feared germ on the planet was not HIV, but the virus that causes poliomyelitis, or polio. Polio destroys nerve cells, cruelly paralyzing and often killing its victims. More than 80 percent of polio patients were below the age of five.

The first major polio epidemic struck the United States in the summer of 1916. By the end of the summer, 27,000 people were paralyzed and 9,000 were dead. The virus struck again year after year, mainly in July and August. In 1952, there were 52,000 cases and 3,300 deaths. During "polio season," parents kept their children inside, leaving playgrounds deserted and swimming pools empty. "You could have a normal child one day and the next day a child who was dead or paralyzed for life," said Martin Blaser, chair of medicine at New York University.

By the late 1940s, researchers learned that the polio virus was spread directly from person to person through contact with microscopic particles of saliva or solid human waste. But it was not until 1952 that Jonas Salk, a young researcher at the University of Pittsburgh, developed an experimental vaccine to combat the polio virus.

By 1954, Salk received government approval for mass testing of the vaccine. The Salk vaccine was officially declared safe on April 12, 1955. Over the following months, more than 650,000 children in grades 1 to 3 were vaccinated across the country. During the first three years of widespread use of the Salk vaccine (1955–57),

cases of polio in the United States fell by nearly 90 percent. Before 1962, when an oral vaccine developed by Albert Sabin began to be used in the United States, cases of polio had decreased by 95 percent. With the use of those two vaccines, naturally occurring polio virus was wiped out in North and South America and in western Europe.

In 1988, there were 355,000 cases of polio in 125 countries. By the end of 2006, there were just 1,999 cases. Six countries reported polio outbreaks in 2006: Afghanistan, Egypt, India, Niger, Nigeria, and Pakistan. The World Health Organization has a goal of completely eliminating polio worldwide through the Global Polio Eradication Initiative (GPEI).

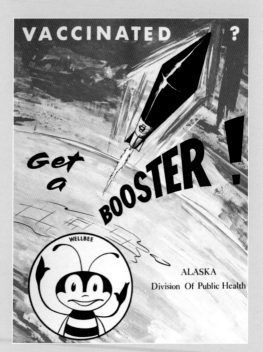

⋀ Once the polio vaccine was approved by the federal government, individual states launched aggressive campaigns designed to publicize and encourage vaccinations.

∧ The gorilla population of the Republic of the Congo, already endangered, has been nearly wiped out by the Ebola virus, with more than 5,500 of the great apes found dead from the disease.

Sharing Disease

When animals and humans share a disease it can create an even greater risk for pandemic. The term zoonosis describes the somewhat common event when a virus which has previously only affected animals mutates so that humans become sick from it as well. It is also possible for viruses which have typically only affected people to change and pose health risks for animals. This type of illness is described as anthrozoonotic and includes influenza, measles, and tuberculosis in addition to many others. Today, field researchers and scientists recognize that science needs to look at a bigger picture to understand the future. As our population grows, the borders between animal and human habitats become less defined. We live in overlapping territories, exposing each other to new and different germs. Scientists no longer study just how sick human beings can become from animals. They study the opposite to understand the way viruses endure and cause damage to their victims. Diseases cannot be separated by animal or human labels. A global approach to health and research will be necessary so the fragile balance of our world can be maintained.

A Very Real Threat

CHAPTER 5

A genetically altered virus creates fear

Most people know the story of Frankenstein's monster. Dr. Frankenstein hoped to create an artificial human from a collection of body parts dug up from graves. He sewed the creature together, ran some electricity through it, and watched it come alive. But instead of creating a normal man, Frankenstein ended up creating a killer monster that terrorized the countryside.

The tale of Dr. Frankenstein, of course, is fiction, a story written by Mary Shelley in 1818. But scientists today are capable of creating a real

< Field workers who identify possible bioterror threats wear protective suits while investigating the presence of chemicals in places where there could be a danger to the general public.

monster, or Frankengerm! In the wrong hands, it has the potential to kill far more people than Mary Shelley's monster ever could.

Mousepox Virus

It began in 2001 in Australia. A research team there was trying to alter the virus that causes mousepox, a close relative of the human smallpox virus. They were hoping to develop a means of pest control by creating a virus that would prevent mice from reproducing.

The scientists inserted a gene into the mousepox virus that they hoped would cause the virus to stimulate a mouse's immune system to reject mouse eggs, making a female mouse unable to produce babies.

Mousepox normally causes only mild symptoms in mice, but the altered virus turned into a raging killer. The virus attacked the immune system of the mice, destroying their ability to fight viruses, much as HIV attacks the human immune system, only much faster.

"It's surprising how very, very bad the virus is," said Ann Hill, a researcher at the University of Portland (Oregon).

The new virus wiped out 100 percent of the laboratory mice in only nine days. Even worse, it proved unnaturally resistant to any attempts to vaccinate the mice.

∧ Children affected with smallpox at the Bihari Relief Camp in Dacca, Bangladesh. Unsanitary facilities at these refugee camps made the outbreak of diseases more difficult to treat and control. Fortunately, smallpox was wiped out in 1977.

Bioweapons

Fortunately, the new supervirus did not escape the laboratory to cause mayhem on the order of Dr. Frankenstein's monster. But the 2001 experiment worries scientists and others for what it suggests for the future. The chief concern is that terrorists or hostile governments could use the technique discovered by the Australian scientists to inject a similar gene into the human smallpox virus. The altered smallpox germ would be a dangerous "bioweapon," a genetically engineered virus designed to spread quickly, sickening and killing many people in a very short span of time. Such an epidemic would be extremely difficult to prevent.

The Australian experiment is "a good way to show how to alter smallpox to make it more [destructive]," said Ken Alibek, an expert in germ warfare.

In 2003, Mark Buller of the University of St. Louis and his team deliberately re-created the 2001 Australian work with mousepox. Buller also performed the same experiment with cowpox, a virus that affects cows, but can also affect humans. Buller, who was funded by the U.S. government, told the *New Scientist* magazine in 2003 that his work was necessary to explore what bioterrorists might do. If a potential bioterror threat can be created in a laboratory, scientists need to be able to develop defenses against it.

An Age-Old Disease

Smallpox has been around for thousands of years. Egyptian mummies show that ancient Egyptians had the disease. The virus that causes the disease is the variola virus, a germ so small that 1,000 of them linked together cover only the width of a human hair. Even though it is tiny, the variola virus packs a monster punch. It causes high fever, oozing blisters, and death, especially in children. It is also the only disease that scientists have succeeded in wiping out. In 1967, the World Health Organization launched a campaign to wipe out the disease through inoculation. The campaign worked. The world's last natural case of smallpox occurred on October 27, 1977, in the African nation of Somalia. Today the "wild" smallpox virus exists in only two places: a high-security lab in the United States and one in Russia. U.S. experts fear, however, that security could be breached and some of the remaining virus could be obtained by terrorists.

∨ Scientists who study viruses hope to use their knowledge to prevent possible future outbreaks of bioterrorism.

∧ Staff members at a conference on global security in Singapore in 2007 pose with signs and a model of a new smallpox vaccine called Imvamune, designed to combat strains of smallpox virus that might have been modified and potentially employed by bioterrorists.

The natural smallpox virus was wiped out through vaccinations. But, as the Australian researchers found out, the altered mousepox virus is almost impossible to vaccinate against. An altered smallpox virus might also be difficult to vaccinate against. The result of releasing such a killer virus would be catastrophic. The germ spreads like a cold virus, passing from person to person on droplets that are emitted when a person coughs or sneezes.

"The possibility [of a smallpox bioweapon] scares me," virologist Don Francis told *USA Today*. "It's a dangerous disease, and we have little immunity." Francis and others, however, believe that such a bioattack could be contained with careful international cooperation and planning and by using the resources of modern science. No one, however, is absolutely sure.

Black ICE

The threat of a bioterror attack involving an altered smallpox virus was the subject of a January 2007 exercise involving the U.S. government and the government of Switzerland. The exercise was called "Black ICE" (Bioterrorism International Coordination Exercise).

As part of Black ICE, a fake smallpox attack was imagined, with terrorists traveling by airplane in Asia, Europe, and North America. The imaginary terrorists infected themselves with the smallpox virus, flew to a particular destination, and then proceeded to visit a heavily attended outdoor event in a major city. Throughout the experiment, 357 individuals were "infected" in 17 nations with the smallpox bioweapon. The challenge was to plan how governments would react to contain the pandemic and stop it.

Germs, whether or not they are released by terrorists, do not respect borders. As part of the exercise, the United States and Switzerland recommended that all international organizations, including the United Nations, develop ways of tracking the spread of the disease from its first discovery. The two countries also recommended that health officials from all nations should work together to lessen the threat and that international media organizations should inform people of the disease and how to protect against it.

Many Americans are already worried about bioterrorism. A UPI-Zogby International poll of 10,258 Americans taken in February 2007 asked which global health risk poses the greatest threat. The threat of bioterrorism attacks was cited by nearly 34 percent as the top risk. "Not sure" was second (26.1 percent). Bird flu was third at 18.6 percent, followed by the threat of HIV/AIDS at 11.4 percent.

V **Timothy Hannon explains how the Lightweight Epidemiology Advanced Detection and Emergency Response System (LEADERS) can detect disease outbreaks by scanning hospitals' electronic records and alert officials to bioterror outbreaks through cell phones, e-mail, and pagers.**

Bugs Fly Free

CHAPTER 6

Germs travel the globe in hours

We live in an age of speed. People are used to fast food, fast cars, fast computers, and fast travel. According to the World Health Organization however, we will also have to get used to fast germs. While speed has transformed and improved our lives, it has also made it possible for germs to travel around the globe in less than a day.

At the time of the Black Death, it took years for the bacterium that causes bubonic plague to travel from Asia to northern Europe. Today the same bacterium could make the same journey in an hour

⟨ Facilities at a pigeon farm in China are disinfected against bird flu in an effort to prevent local outbreaks from becoming an epidemic.

or so. A germ lurking in a muddy ditch in an Indian village as the sun comes up could find itself on a plate in a New York City restaurant at dinnertime.

This fact alarms the scientists at WHO and health officials everywhere. Not only are new infectious diseases such as AIDS, Ebola, and bird flu emerging at an "unprecedented rate," according to WHO, but humans are moving about the globe at a feverish pace. Travel by planes, trains, and ships means that these diseases have the potential to infect vast parts of Earth very quickly, sweeping across continents in just a few months.

Panic at the Airport

The rapid way germs can spread contributed to "the big tuberculosis scare of 2007," as newspapers called it. Tuberculosis (TB) is a highly contagious disease caused by a bacterium. The bacterium causes small rounded swellings, or tubercles, to form on mucous membranes, linings in the parts of the body where air passes. They can appear on any mucus membrane, but most often affect the lungs. The bacteria can eventually destroy the lungs, leading to death.

Antibiotics—substances that kill bacteria—have been used for many years to cure TB patients. But a new and very dangerous strain of TB

▽ An Air China Boeing 777 jet sits grounded at Beijing airport in 2003. Chinese airlines experienced huge losses that year when passengers alarmed by the SARS outbreak avoided air travel, causing business to fall off by 80 percent.

bacteria has emerged that existing antibiotics cannot kill. Known as drug-resistant TB, the strain has now been detected in 37 countries, alarming health officials.

> ∧ High-speed travel, especially in populous countries like China, can contribute to the spread of infectious diseases.

In January 2007, Andrew Speaker, an Atlanta lawyer, learned

∧ It was feared that Andrew Speaker was contagious and harmful to others when he traveled from the United States to Europe and Canada with a positive tuberculosis diagnosis.

he had TB. In May, doctors believed that he had a highly drug-resistant strain of the disease. Soon afterward, Speaker boarded an airplane flight to Europe for a business trip. He then returned from Europe to Canada. Health

officials at the Centers for Disease Control (CDC) in Atlanta were afraid that Speaker would spread the disease to everyone he came in contact with on the planes and in Europe. From Canada, Speaker drove across the U.S.-Canadian border. A U.S. border patrol agent, disregarding a government warning to hold Speaker and call health authorities, allowed him back into the United States.

When he returned to Atlanta, Speaker was put into a hospital. In a TV interview, he apologized to everyone for what he had done. "I'm very sorry for any grief or pain that I have caused anyone," he said from an isolation room in the National

Jewish Hospital in Denver, where the most difficult TB cases are treated. He said the CDC doctors never warned him not to travel, although the doctors said they did tell him. He also said that he did not think he could have infected anyone else with the disease.

How many people were put at risk? As it turns out, no one. Doctors later found that Speaker had been misdiagnosed: he did not have a severely dangerous form of TB. Everyone breathed a sigh of relief, but Speaker's case highlighted the huge problem of trying to contain a serious disease in an age of fast air travel around the world.

The SARS Scare

Four years earlier, in 2003, a new virus that causes severe acute respiratory syndrome (SARS) had created a more serious international panic. SARS is a very contagious illness with an incubation rate of one week before symptoms occur. One of the first known cases of SARS afflicted a 72-year-old man from Beijing, China's capital city. The man took at least one plane trip before he experienced the symptoms that characterize SARS. During the plane trip, however, he likely infected 22 fellow passengers, many of whom later took different planes headed in different directions.

∧ In Hong Kong, pedestrians walking along a downtown overpass wear face masks to protect them from the SARS virus after nearly 300 people died of the disease in 2003.

Quarantine!

Quarantine is the forced separation of sick and diseased people from healthy people. It is a method that has been used to fight the spread of disease for thousands of years. Even though early peoples did not know how microbes cause disease, they were aware that contact with diseased people spread illness.

∧ A sketch illustrating people being taken by force to an isolation hospital in Milwaukee, Wisconsin in 1894, during a citywide smallpox outbreak.

In the 1400s, people still attributed disease to a number of incorrect factors such as bad air, sin, and even demons. But in Venice, Italy, and other cities by the sea, they knew that disease and plague seemed to occur when ships from other areas, particularly the Middle East, came into the harbor. This led the city fathers of Venice to develop the first real system of quarantine. Ships arriving in Venice had to remain in the harbor for *quarantina*, or 40 days, before docking. *Quarantina* is the origin of the word quarantine.

Asia also had quarantine laws. As early as the 600s, China had a well-established policy for quarantining plague-stricken sailors and foreign travelers who had arrived in Chinese ports.

The general quarantine system based on Venice's was the model for all quarantines until the late 1800s when the discoveries by French scientist Louis Pasteur and the German physician Robert Koch led to better understanding about the specific causes of diseases and how they are spread. Quarantines came to be thought of as cruel or immoral as new ways of treating illness arose and the public became more educated about disease.

With the emergence of new diseases, however, antiquated ways of thinking sometimes take hold. In the early 1990s when HIV and AIDS began to spread, a lack of scientific knowledge and public education about the disease led some to suggest quarantine for those who were afflicted.

Even today, quarantines are the first defense against the rise of such diseases as Ebola, bird flu, and SARS, all of which can easily be spread through air travel. Quarantines have been used at international airports to isolate suspected carriers of bird flu. On November 12, 2007, New Zealand quarantined 223 people on a Korean airliner after a South Korean passenger displayed symptoms of bird flu.

This created a nightmare for health officials trying to track down the virus and quarantine, or medically isolate, those who might pass it on.

Officials found fresh cases of SARS in Hong Kong, China, and Canada, although it is unclear whether they stemmed from the man in Beijing. Luckily, SARS proved to be less infectious than officials first believed. Health officials were able to isolate the virus quickly. Still, SARS ended up killing several hundred people.

What keeps health officials awake at night, however, is what will happen if and when a truly contagious virus or bacterium mutates into a serious worldwide health threat. How will officials keep the threat contained in an age when germs can hitch rides on supersonic jets and travel rapidly all over the planet?

Because of this risk, greater international cooperation among health officials, governments, and scientists is essential, says Margaret Chan, the director general of WHO. The organization has set up guidelines allowing scientists to alert health officials quickly about new threats and new diseases. If officials know what to look for, they may be able to prevent the spread of disease from one country or region to another. If all concerned can act as quickly as the germ itself can spread, perhaps the disease can be contained.

Computers to the Rescue

At the end of November 2006, scientists and computer experts from around the globe gathered in Boca Raton, Florida. Their goal: to develop a worldwide computer system to track the spread of infectious disease, particularly bird flu. They represented WHO, CDC, and other organizations that are looking for ways to establish a worldwide computer net. The net would search for reported outbreaks of disease anywhere in the world. The reports would be fed into powerful computers that would combine data on world travel patterns, the spread of similar diseases, and other health information. Health officials in New York or London, for

∧ Dr. Margaret Chan, director-general of the World Health Organization, is an expert in pandemic outbreaks. In 1994, as the director of health in Hong Kong, she oversaw the city's response to the avian flu epidemic. In 2003, she effectively managed the outbreak of the SARS epidemic in China.

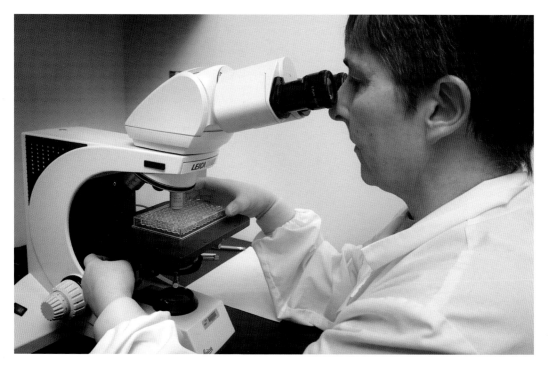

∧ Scientists rely on new technologies to combat the growing number of deadly germs in the world today. A researcher at the CDC utilizes dark-field microscopy, a method that uses indirect light to view a specimen.

instance, aware of an outbreak of bird flu in Indonesia, would be able to estimate how, where, and how fast the disease would spread. Such a pooling of information at computer speed would be a great help to health officials and could save many lives.

An even bigger boost to world health might come from Project Checkmate, a plan by IBM and the Scripps Research Institute to build the world's most powerful supercomputer. The new Blue Gene computer would be dedicated to disease research. It would be able to do 1.2 quadrillion computations a second. (A quadrillion is one thousand times one trillion!) That would allow the computer to

model how selected viruses mutate their genes, making them into killers. The knowledge would allow scientists to make new vaccines almost as fast as viruses change.

Will supercomputers, powerful microscopes, and the efforts of scientists all over the world be able to prevent the next pandemic? Will the flu virus, Ebola, and superbugs be squashed by the powerful forces of science and technology?

Hopefully. But even with all our knowledge and resources, humans are up against a group of determined, clever, and very ancient enemies that have proved their ability to survive and kill again and again.

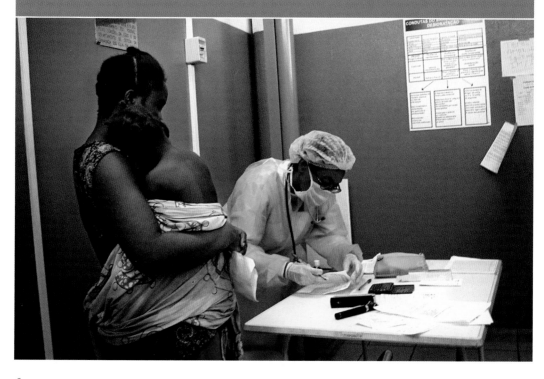

∧ A 2005 outbreak of Marburg disease in Luanda brought many people to the hospital to be tested for the deadly virus. Scientists are hoping that future epidemics can be prevented through satellite tracking of species that host the virus, and biohacking, the practice of creating a mutated form of the virus in order to study it and find a cure.

NASA (National Aeronautics and Space Administration) currently monitors 14 orbiting satellites that more infectious disease scientists turn to every day. In addition to watching for viral outbreaks, the information collected on climate change will be used to understand how different germs change and thrive in new conditions. Attention is currently focused on the disease malaria, which affects more than 300 million people around the world. Satellites transmit information on how the environment affects the spread of malaria. The goal is to prevent or restrict the size of outbreaks by following the early warning signs provided by the data gathered in space. It is also hoped that satellite technology will enable scientists to determine if an infectious outbreak is the result of bioterrorism or a naturally occurring incident.

Biohacking is the newest direction scientists are taking to investigate viruses. Re-engineering the makeup of germs like HIV leads researchers to create new viruses for study. These man-made viruses are manipulated to learn how they respond to different treatments. The results will help medical doctors treat similar, naturally occurring viruses.

Glossary

antibiotic — a chemical used to kill an infectious organism

antibody — a protein produced by certain white blood cells that attacks foreign substances in the body

B cell — a type of lymphocyte that produces antibodies; part of the human immune system

bacteriophage — a virus that attacks and lives in a certain bacterium

bacterium —a microscopic, one-celled organism that does not have a nucleus; plural: bacteria

DNA (deoxyribonucleic acid) — material found inside a living cell that contains the codes needed to build proteins and carries the genetic information about an organism

electron microscope — a microscope that uses electron rays instead of light rays to produce very high magnification

epidemic — when a disease affects many people in a local area where the sickness is not usually found

gene — a minute part of a chromosome that holds genetic information and determines a specific characteristic of an organism

HIV (human immunodeficiency virus) — the virus that causes AIDS

immune system — the system of antibodies and white blood cells that recognizes, attacks, and destroys foreign substances that enter the body

inoculation — to introduce a substance into the body that will produce or increase immunity to a disease

lymphocyte — a type of white blood cell that is primarily responsible for the development of immunity; includes B cells and T cells

memory cell — a B cell or T cell that has been exposed to a foreign substance and can instantly respond to the same substance at a later time

microbe — a germ, or microorganism

microbiologist — a scientist who studies microscopic life

molecule — the smallest particle into which an element can be divided without changing its properties

mutation — a change within a gene or chromosome resulting in a new characteristic that is inherited

nucleotide — a chemical building block of DNA and RNA

pandemic — a widespread epidemic that affects people in different countries or regions

pheromone — in biology, a chemical used for communication

plasmid — a small circle of DNA in the cells of bacteria or viruses

protein — a substance containing nitrogen; the major structural building block of animal and plant cells

RNA (ribonucleic acid) — an acid found in living cells that takes the place of DNA in some viruses

SARS — severe acute respiratory syndrome

T cell — a type of lymphocyte that regulates the response of the immune system or kills certain types of cells

tubercle — small, rounded swelling caused by the tuberculosis bacterium

vaccine — a substance made from killed or weakened viruses or bacteria used to inoculate a person in order to prevent a disease and produce immunity to it

virus — a disease-producing particle composed of genetic material covered with a protein coat; a virus can reproduce only in a living cell

Bibliography

Books

Farrell, Jeanette. *Invisible Enemies: Stories of Infectious Disease*. New York: Farrar, Straus & Giroux, 2005.

Giblin, James Cross. *When Plague Strikes: The Black Death, Smallpox, AIDS*. New York: Harper Collins Children's Books, 1996.

Martinez-Palomo, Adolfo. *Invisible ABCs: Exploring the World of Microbes*. New York: Journal of Public Health Policy, 2006.

Thomas, Peggy. *Bacteria and Viruses*. New York: Lucent Books, 2004.

Articles

Quammen, David. "Deadly Contact." NATIONAL GEOGRAPHIC (October 2007): 78–105.

Further Reading

Brunelle, Lynn and Marc Gave (Editors). *Viruses* (Discovery Channel School Science). Chicago, Illinois: Gareth Stevens Publishing, 2003.

Maczulak, Anne E. *The Five-Second Rule and Other Myths About Germs: What Everyone Should Know About Bacteria, Viruses, Mold, and Mildew*. New York: Thunder's Mouth Press, 2007.

Thomas, Peggy. *Bacteria and Viruses* (The Lucent Library of Science and Technology). San Diego, California: Lucent Books, 2004.

On the Web

BioMEDIA ASSOCIATES Learning Programs for Biology Education
http://ebiomedia.com/gall/bacteria/

Digital Learning Center for Microbial Ecology
http://commtechlab.msu.edu/sites/dlc-me/zoo/

Molecular Expressions: Optical Microscopy Primer
http://micro.magnet.fsu.edu/primer/virtual/virtual.html

Rader's Biology4Kids Digital Learning Center for Microbial Ecology
http://www.biology4kids.com/files/micro_main.html

The Microbiology Information Portal
http://www.microbes.info/

Index

Boldface indicates illustrations.

About the Author

Charles Piddock is a former editor in chief of Weekly Reader corporation, publisher of sixteen classroom magazines for schools from pre-K through high school, including *Current Events, Current Science,* and *Teen Newsweek*. In his career with Weekly Reader, he has written and edited hundreds of articles for young people of all ages on world and national affairs, science, literature, and other topics. Piddock also served as a Peace Corps volunteer in rural West Bengal, India.

About the Consultant

Caryn Oryniak studied molecular biology and virology at Lehigh University before becoming a medical technologist where she examined the blood and body fluids of sick patients, looking for infectious organisms. She spent much of her career running labs that create and examine products designed to kill bacteria and viruses. She holds a patent for one of these types of formulations, which are used to help keep our daily environment safe, and to reduce the spread of infections. She currently works as a research manager at a New Jersey manufacturing company.

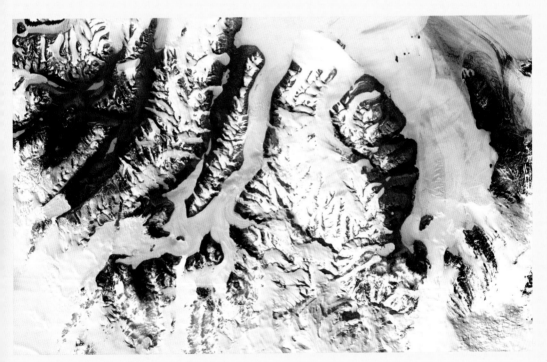

Λ The McMurdo Dry Valleys in Antarctica are reservoirs of bacteria that scientists study in hopes of providing information about diseases and their treatment.

Founded in 1888, the National Geographic Society is one of the largest nonprofit scientific and educational organizations in the world. It reaches more than 285 million people worldwide each month through its official journal, NATIONAL GEOGRAPHIC, and its four other magazines; the National Geographic Channel; television documentaries; radio programs; films; books; videos and DVDs; maps; and interactive media. National Geographic has funded more than 8,000 scientific research projects and supports an education program combating geographic illiteracy.

For more information, please call 1-800-NGS LINE (647-5463) or write to the following address:

National Geographic Society
1145 17th Street N.W., Washington, D.C.
20036-4688 U.S.A.

Visit us online at
www.nationalgeographic.com/books

For librarians and teachers:
www.ngchildrensbooks.com

More for kids from National Geographic:
kids.nationalgeographic.com

For information about special discounts for bulk purchases, please contact National Geographic Books Special Sales: ngspecsales@ngs.org

For rights or permissions inquiries, please contact National Geographic Books Subsidiary Rights: ngbookrights@ngs.org

Library of Congress Cataloging-in-Publication Data available upon request

Hardcover ISBN: 978-1-4263-0357-9
Library ISBN: 978-1-4263-0263-3

Printed in China

Book design by Dan Banks, Project Design Company

**Published by the
National Geographic Society**
John M. Fahey, Jr., *President and Chief Executive Officer;* Gilbert M. Grosvenor, *Chairman of the Board;* Tim T. Kelly, *President, Global Media Group;* Nina D. Hoffman, *Executive Vice President; President, Book Publishing Group*

Prepared by the Book Division
Nancy Laties Feresten, *Vice President, Editor in Chief, Children's Books*
Bea Jackson, *Director of Design and Illustrations, Children's Books*
Amy Shields, *Executive Editor, Series, Children's Books*

Staff for This Book
Virginia Ann Koeth, *Editor*
Jim Hiscott, *Art Director*
Lori Epstein, *Illustrations Editor*
Lewis R. Bassford, *Production Manager*
Grace Hill, *Associate Managing Editor*
Stuart Armstrong, *Graphics*
Jennifer A. Thornton, *Managing Editor*
R. Gary Colbert, *Production Director*
Susan Borke, *Legal and Business Affairs*

Manufacturing and Quality Management
Christopher A. Liedel, *Chief Financial Officer*
Phillip L. Schlosser, *Vice President*
Chris Brown, *Technical Director*
Nicole Elliott, *Manager*

Photo Credits
Front: Bobby Yip/ Reuters/ Corbis
Back & Spine: Mehau Kulyk/ Photo Researchers, Inc.
Back Icon: CC Studio/ Photo Researchers, Inc.

AP = Associated Press; 1, AP; 2-3, Dimas Ardian/Getty Images; 4, David Lucas/Getty Images; 6, CDC/James Gathany; 8, courtesy of the consultant; 9, *National Geographic*, October 2007: 93; 12-13, National Museum of Health & Medicine, Armed Forces Institute of Pathology Reeve15943; 14, (top) CDC/Cynthia Goldsmith; 14, (bottom) 15, National Museum of Health & Medicine, Armed Forces Institute of Pathology Reeve15943; 16, 17, 18, (top) AP; 18 (bottom), Carrier/Bloomberg News/Landov; 19, 20, 21, 22, AP; 24-25, A. Barry Dowsett/Photo Researchers, Inc.; 26, ERIC ERBE/SCIENCE PHOTO LIBRARY; 27, NIBSC/SCIENCE PHOTO LIBRARY; 28, CDC/James Gathany; 30-31, Chris Sattlberger/Photo Researchers, Inc.; 32, IAN BODDY/SCIENCE PHOTO LIBRARY; 33, NAASHON ZALK/Bloomberg News/Landov; 34, Bibliotheque Nationale, Paris, France, Archives Charmet/The Bridgeman Art Library; 35, National Institutes of Health/National Cancer Institute; 36-37, Photos.com; 38 (top), CDC;38 (bottom), AP; 39 (left and right), CDC; 40, (top) AP; 40 (bottom), CDC/P. Rouquet; 41, Istock; 42, CDC; 43, Photos.com; 44-45, Istock; 46, Bernard Pierre Wolff/Photo Researchers, Inc.; 47, Istock; 48, Xinhua/Landov; 49, AP; 50-51, China Photos/Getty Image; 52, 53, (top) AP; 53 (bottom), NATIONAL JEWISH MEDICAL AND RESEARCH CENTER/UPI/Landov; 54, AP; 55, Library of Congress; 56, 57 AP; 58, National Oceanic and Atmospheric Administration's (NOAA) Advanced Very High Resolution Radiometer (AVHRR); 60, CDC; 63, NASA;

Front cover: A mourner wears a mask during the funeral of a SARS victim in China.

Back cover: E. coli bacteria

Page 1: A scientist inspects bacteria found inside a ventilation unit in order to determine whether bioterrorism played a role in the presence of pathogens found in Boston in 2001.

Pages 2–3: A young girl receives an oral vaccine.

A Creative Media Applications, Inc. Production
Editor: Susan Madoff
Copy Editor: Laurie Lieb
Design and Production: Luís Leon and Fabia Wargin